SAY
IT
AGAIN

Brian Cassie

Illustrated by David Mooney

ᐱᐱ Charlesbridge

Some creatures, from Peru to Ghana,
And Madagascar to Guyana,
Have names that have a double sound.
Here are a few that we have found:

An Aye-Aye hiding in a tree
Is just as strange as it can be—
With big, round eyes and long, thin toes,
Ragged ears, and a short, flat nose.

DIK DIK

Within the brush two Dik-Diks hide
And stand in silence, side by side.
Above them noisy bulbuls call,
But Dik-Diks make no noise at all.

CARACARA

A Caracara flies with ease
Across the fields, above the trees.
Its shadow falls upon a mouse
That might be safer in its house.

Off Bora Bora or Cape Cod,
The Mola Mola is quite odd.
A stranger fish is hard to find:
It's long up front and short behind.

MOLA MOLA

When twilight falls upon the land,
And shadows stretch across the sand,
The Coro-Coros fill the sky
With colors that electrify.

In muddy waters, dark and dim,
Two Susus on a morning swim
Will sometimes rise straight up and try
To see each other eye to eye.

SUSU

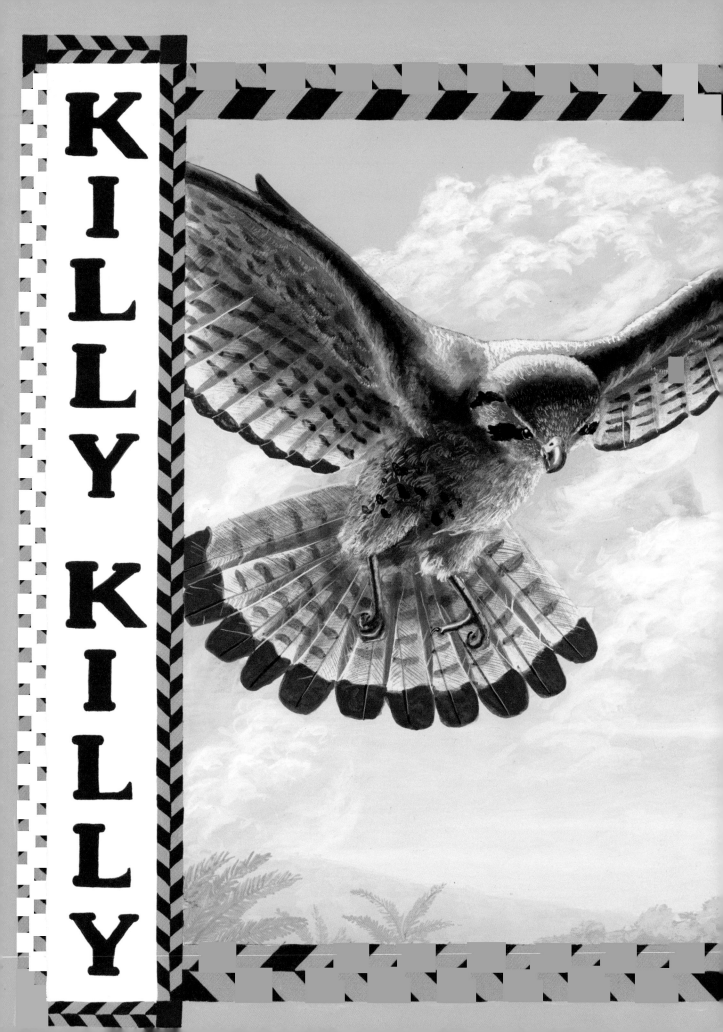

KILLY KILLY

It sometimes does great flying stunts,
But when the Killy-Killy hunts,
It beats its wings with all its might
And stays in one place, like a kite.

CHICO CHICO

Awake and active since first light,
This monkey has an appetite.
A katydid is the ideal
Chico Chico lunchtime meal.

Babas often like to float
In places that are quite remote.
With ruby eyes, they look around
Both in the water and on the ground.

BABA

Most hummingbirds are very small,
And some seem barely there at all.
In order to be better seen,
The tiny Frou-Frou's crest shines green.

FROU FROU

Up high among the forest boughs
Live tiny bugs and great Wow-Wows.
And when the Wow-Wows first awake,
Their hollers make the forest shake.

WONGA WONGA

In forests deep and dark and green,
At dawn and dusk and in between,
A handsome spotted-bellied bird,
The Wonga-Wonga, can be heard.

Where do these animals live?

Frou-Frou

Coro-Coro

Chico Chico

Mola Mola

Caracara

Killy-Killy

Baba

Susu

Dik-Dik

Wow-Wow

Aye-Aye

Wonga-Wonga

Where do animals get their names?

When an animal is discovered and classified by a scientist, it is given a scientific name. For some animals, everyone uses the scientific name. One well-known scientific name is *Tyrannosaurus rex*. Usually, though, people use other names when they talk about an animal. These names are called common names. Some animals have only one common name. Some animals have a lot of them. Common names can be based on the way an animal looks, where it lives, the sounds it makes, or other things people notice about it. Common names for animals exist in all languages. The animals in this book all have names, either common or scientific, with a double sound. There are many more such creatures to be found, including the Dodo, Cuckoo, Gangang, Joggle-Joggle, Lumba Lumba, Nunu, and Pong-Pong!

Aye-Aye

Madagascar, a huge island off the east coast of Africa, is home to this strange creature, the weirdest-looking and weirdest-acting of all the lemurs. Aye-Ayes are named for their echoing calls. They tap trunks of trees with their long, skinny middle fingers and listen for insects under the wood. When they hear one, they dig it out with their fingers and their sharp teeth.

Dik-Dik

Dik-Diks are very small African antelopes. They are almost always found in or near the shelter of shrubs and other vegetation. Female Dik-Diks are larger than males. Dik-Diks are usually quiet and shy, but if one is startled as it is feeding it will jump away in a zigzag pattern, calling "dik dik" as it bounds to safety.

Caracara

There are ten kinds of Caracaras in the world. All of them are raptors, or birds of prey, and all of them live in North or South America or Cuba. Many Caracaras find their food, including insects, small mammals, and carrion, on the ground. The Crested Caracara shown in this book has the largest range of any Caracara. Caracaras are named for their calls.

Mola Mola

Ocean Sunfish is a common name for the fish with the scientific name *Mola mola*. This fish likes to sun itself by swimming on its side. In rare cases, the Mola Mola can grow to be eleven feet long and may weigh as much as two thousand pounds. Mola Molas live in both tropical and cool ocean waters around the world.

Coro-Coro

In the Caroni Swamp in Trinidad, Coro-Coros fly to their roosts in the mangrove trees as the sun is setting. Their swirling flight is a great spectacle in northern South America. The Coro-Coro is also called the Scarlet Ibis. It is related to herons and egrets and has a long, curved bill, perfect for probing for food in swamps and marshes.

Susu

There are many types of dolphins in the world, but very few of them live in freshwater. Susus, however, live only in freshwater rivers. They have very small eyes for dolphins, but even if they had much larger eyes, they could not see very well in the muddy waters in which they usually swim. The name Susu comes from one of the sounds they make when surfacing to breathe.

Killy-Killy

Killy-Killy is a name used by Caribbean islanders for the American Kestrel. A small falcon, the Killy-Killy sometimes hunts birds, mice, lizards, and insects by hovering over open land and then dropping down upon its prey. Its "killy-killy-killy" call is commonly heard when it is in flight.

Chico Chico

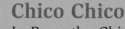

In Peru, the Chico Chico lives among the thick vines that grow in the Amazon rain forest. Even with its fantastic white mustache, the Chico Chico is hard to see hiding among the lianas. In other areas the Chico Chico is called the Emperor Tamarin.

Baba

There are no alligators in South America, but there are Babas. The Baba is also known as the Spectacled Caiman. It is a close relative of the alligator and the crocodile, but its snout is more pointed than an alligator's and less pointed than a crocodile's. It can grow to be over ten feet long. The bellowing roar of a Baba is a sound that is hard to forget.

Frou-Frou

Frou-frou is a French word that describes a rustling sound. In French-speaking Caribbean islands, the Antillean Crested Hummingbird is called the Frou-Frou. It is one of the world's smallest birds. But even at just three and a half inches it can drive much larger birds, including hawks, from its nesting territory. The Frou-Frou gets its name from the whirring sound of its busy wings.

Wow-Wow

The Wow-Wow, or Silvery Gibbon, lives on the island of Java and is named for its loud early-morning calls. Gibbons are the most acrobatic of all the apes. They use their long arms to swing themselves through their rain-forest homes. In addition to being wonderful athletes, gibbons are tremendous singers, and their voices ring through the forest canopy.

Wonga-Wonga

The Wonga-Wonga is a large, beautiful pigeon that lives only in the rain forests and other woodlands of Australia. It is also called the Wonga Pigeon. Wonga-Wongas feed on the ground and rest up in the trees. They are named for their far-carrying "wonga wonga" calls. If you visit the Wonga-Wonga's habitat, you have a good chance of seeing one, since they are quite common.

*To my beautiful daughter Jane, who
wrote the Aye-Aye poem, and to Dodos—
those wonderful birds that would be such a
natural treasure if only they were still with us
—B.C.*

*To the young naturalists and artists
who are just discovering their world
—D.M.*

With thanks to Dr. Kevin J. McGowan of the Cornell Vertebrate Collections, Cornell University; Alan Mootnick of the International Center for Gibbon Studies; and Dr. Victor G. Springer of the National Museum of Natural History's Division of Fishes, for their review of illustrations and text, and to editor Kelly Swanson of Charlesbridge Publishing.

Published by Charlesbridge Publishing
85 Main Street, Watertown, MA 02472
(617) 926-0329
www.charlesbridge.com

Library of Congress Cataloging-in-Publication Data
Cassie, Brian, 1953-
Say it again/Brian Cassie; illustrated by David Mooney.
p. cm.
Summary: Rhyming text describes 12 animals with double names, like aye-aye,
chico chico, killy-killy, and mola mola.
ISBN 0-88106-341-X (reinforced for library use)
ISBN 0-88106-342-8 (softcover)
1. Zoology—Nomenclature—Juvenile literature. [1. Animals. 2. Vocabulary.]
I. Mooney, David, ill. II. Title.
QL354.C27   2000
590—dc21   99-13394

Printed in the United States of America

(hc) 10 9 8 7 6 5 4 3 2 1
(sc) 10 9 8 7 6 5 4 3 2 1

The illustrations in this book were done in acrylic paint on illustration board.
The display type and text type were set in Obelisk and Slimbach.
Color separations were made by ArtScans Studio, Inc., Manhattan Beach, California.
Printed and bound by Worzalla Publishing Company, Stevens Point, Wisconsin
Production supervision by Brian G. Walker
Designed by Diane M. Earley
This book was printed on recycled paper.